Triple Twelve

poems by

Michael Borth

Finishing Line Press
Georgetown, Kentucky

Triple Twelve

Copyright © 2023 by Michael Borth
ISBN 979-8-88838-214-1 First Edition
All rights reserved under International and Pan-American Copyright Conventions. No part of this book may be reproduced in any manner whatsoever without written permission from the publisher, except in the case of brief quotations embodied in critical articles and reviews.

ACKNOWLEDGMENTS

"The Infinite Afternoon" published by *SELFFUCK*
"The Ultrasound" published by *DFL Lit*

Publisher: Leah Huete de Maines
Editor: Christen Kincaid
Cover Art: Jerry Pena
Author Photo: Daisy Hsieh
Cover Design: Elizabeth Maines McCleavy

Order online: www.finishinglinepress.com
also available on amazon.com

Author inquiries and mail orders:
Finishing Line Press
PO Box 1626
Georgetown, Kentucky 40324
USA

Table of Contents

The Diver Silhouetted By Manta Rays 1

When The Hand Becomes A Harp 2

The Chrome The Cherry 3

Leave Yourself 4

The Infinite Afternoon 6

Parisian Tombstones 7

Expect Drizzle 8

The Neon Highlands 9

The Noise Palace 10

The Beds And Trams Of Lisbon 11

The Broken Ovum 12

The Starblur 13

The Ungulates 14

The Mirrorless Camera 15

She Is Sequestered 16

Metal Ox 18

The Ultrasound 19

The Candy Floss 21

The Black Confetti 22

The Program 23

THE DIVER SILHOUETTED BY MANTA RAYS

The diver silhouetted by manta rays.
The gangster removing razorblades from his face.
The toad that is a turtle and a snail and its viral mucus.
The woman with tinfoil in her hair has gone metal zebra.
The Internet will someday go mall.

The photographer has had enough of it all.
The smoker ashes to the pomp and ceremony.
The drug emits elevator with alacrity.
The lover is a distance in the blue room and window snow.
The encircled variable is the middle doorway of the goddess.

The dinner is populated by the heroic and the hidden.
The mescaline will fly you in cell repair unbidden.
The sutured colossus imbued energies with saffron.
The car is a globe pushed by the brand Diameter.
The pentagonal aesthetes are middle-class reprobates.

The world insists on being where I am not.
The me-sized hole has accumulated itself in The God Squint.
The doorway is clogged by equipment hysterics.
The whispers are too late for the last surviving plant
and the wedding is physically deleted by each and every photograph.

WHEN THE HAND BECOMES A HARP

When the hand becomes a harp
the punishment is elusive but definite,
brown monkeys on the black wires of the village street.
Magenta galaxies are actually born
in cups of thick coffee, in hot dreams of old crushes
in narrow rooms where the small dog
would lie on my chest, napping.

The locals have been drugged with perogies
and I am intrinsic to your idea of suburban weather,
rolling nickel weed in looseleaf paper.
Diluted blue makes a rim of the sky
so it looks below and not above
and we are about to start swimming in the stratosphere,
crossed by the rockets of rich men in tragic arcs.
We never did coke on black tabletops
in the high stable rooms of Hong Kong.

The lucky stars have been found in the corner ash
and I begin to love a spoon, a red match.
Small things happen in the green sheets of the bed.
There is elastic everywhere loosening
and sometimes a woman will jump at your face
on a slender box couch
and you will discuss drinks and snacks
and whether or not you will frequent the kaboom shop.
It is good, we both mean, to be back here with you.

THE CHROME THE CHERRY

Tendential fall of the carbon fluorescent
and the convective overshoot of yet another clique.
The weighted mean and the regression to it,
little black magnets of envy. Another memory cell
of another memory cold and The Catalogue
of only footnote, only reference, lies like
the fiery orb of the zygote emergent. You often,
and must, you must give everything to get nothing
in its correct posture, like a matchstick, like tenements
in the chrome and the cherry of the sundown
where the beers begin to slide, the condensation
meets the sweat, the sweat meets the lipstick,
the straight lines meet the parallax and the vanished,
the salt march of the evening in total collapse. Indigo
wafer of decreasing reminder, a florid infamy,
a contingent brass, nectar running, a quake of sigil
in the aftermath of the concubine, the young nun
fluent in the pleasure box of men, seismic envelope
not yet occurrent, not yet edited by the armchair
and cognac screen, or the lighted honey of the ocean,
we categorize a deity by the garlands we proffered,
occult and common with the sensate lethargic,
the sunglassed face in the tree of small yellow umbrella,
to drop a smoke and to stand a coin, to finally see.

LEAVE YOURSELF

I want to leave myself
in the warehouse district of some filthy party
or the urine channel of the local gutter
or the violet red blush of the desert plateau.

Dispensed into fulcrumed alleys.
Pulling soul from soul in the metro chain,
a layer cake of pale reflections.
I will now miss you
and I will now miss you,
spilled ink and blood cups in the first decan
at the tolling of the twelfth hour of the vibrant bell.

They rode bikes fast over the withered palms,
rusted chains irregular but turning,
but they all fell into the central caldera,
a backhoe on hand, piloted by a smoking boy,
dirt thrown and piled, a sculptor on hand
to make marble souvenirs of the reaching and
soonburied hands, a dirty boombox playing horns
and incessant neurotic note-playing.

I want to leave myself.
I want you to fuck that guy I used to call myself.
While I grate ginger and joke with sarcastic dead winos.
I think at the end of the birth canal there was a warning
sign and on the inside of my skin
they will find claw marks, question marks,
inquisitive hieroglyphic and ra.
My pure and refined laziness will become
the ultimate compassion
as I leave myself, a starvation mannequin
among the puppets and mannequins
of that children's program whose name is forgotten.
There is so much bargaining.
There is so little sleep.
We keep using our minds to change our minds,
gathered together in subway stations, in great coats,
this subway map is from the forties.
A difference of opinion is a difference of option bouquets.
You will keep me in a small velvet bag
and leave me under a Czech railway bench.

THE INFINITE AFTERNOON

The outdoor pingpong table is an avocado moonscape.
The white ants disappear into the gradient flows of guano.
Our stomachs bark like dogs in the hot glare of red spectrum megaflora.
We writhe in snake oil and baby oil and baby black scorpions
turn in the sleeping memory, halobacteria
making a scorchwork of the mahogany empire chair.
The yellow beaks become mottled bananas
in the hot spray of animal magnetism.

We are sore vexed among the lacquer seedlings.
We are tracing shadowcovered cannula shapes in the patio tile.
A sad saxophone is a canonical antiphon among the vapor of the palms.
There are volatile cloudbursts and special tropical tools
and uncanny gypsy moths. Everything can become eye.
Everything can become souled.
The apse remainder is a dim jeweled skull recess
in the regrowth of strong bark.
The spines of the trees are shelled and armored
and telescoping brown bone, flecked.
The jungle is vertebrate and veined running in fractal explosion patterns,
everbranching and reaching in the water dominion and solar gorge.
Magmatic thirst quenched by white circle
and its complexity of myriad veiling.
The green lets emerge a turbulent golden schematic
by way of water prisms. Great orbs burst in the turmeric clay,
in the flesh of imprints and forked methods.
From the resurrected fishnet as hammock comes the ice egg
and geode crack of subliminal rock.
The boy emerges from the skirt of burnt paper
with the body of a white mongoose.
He is a messenger from the long winding passage
of dried and brittle scrolls. The flying insects are rusted machines
in the catastrophic granular of rainbowed drifts.

PARISIAN TOMBSTONES

There is no stamina in the ages,
under heavy blankets in the mist altitude of Nagarkot,
killing spiders all night, by candlelight,
is it uncovered or discovered
it is time to abandon what you thought
everyone thought about you.
Scurry to the shower on the great balcony
in the gentle slumber and stare of the proximal mountains.

She asked me if I had ever had anyone I could trust.
Trust, she said. Trust completely.
Through the champagne she knew the answer was No.
And I said No. Yes I know. I know this about you.
All her wires were torn and twisted and exposed.
She loved Proust and I still love Céline,
for he teaches you floral patch from manure.
I did not sleep but saw the building blocks of life
which are random cartoon items bursting.

I bet you taste like sunshower and marshmallow,
as we drink from the bottles left at Parisian tombstones.

EXPECT DRIZZLE

The eyes have been redacted.
Expect drizzle. She will not be able to see me Saturday
because she has an appointment to attend
an office chair liquidation sale.

In the dream we are happy in the clear water
with the manatee and the float of a killer whale.
It takes months to realize that I should not have quit her.
Like it took me too long to know that I loved you.
We waited out the rain with the older couple,
Christmas Day in Brazil, waiting with groceries.
We knocked our legs together on the rock at the reservoir.

It is a small object that burns through time and space,
which is finally lost in the dark sand with black patterns,
but it tells me it is alive in the future, that this loss
does not matter, it is some kind of sentient child
and also a particle without dimension,
it is another mysterious artifact with no mind for time,
no time for material, nothing to leave behind
and nothing to move toward. It is only everything else
that changes.

THE NEON HIGHLANDS

The vanishing wanderers beneath the Stomp! awning.
Highly recommended Greek wine.
The handpattern can be seen on the broom of the sweeper.
He is sleepless but organizing his mind through high simmer.

She had turned down the engagement in Lahore.
She had one headphone inserted when we met on the roof.
The morning is full of chiseling and engine.
I would take naps in that Maspeth graveyard.

Moving toward the steaming bowl of noodles in the neon wash.
Forgetting you through exponential mantra and hypnosis
and walking gravel inclines in the stone gore of the highlands.
Elaborate off-track betting for who I know will perish next.

Scattering on the granite peaks are the pages of the master haiku.
Following the paths to the bell stations of the foothills.
Whispering to the hands I run together to make clear spark.
Watching myself appear in the foreign language film of the theater.

Stripmall ecstasy and the scientist of shelf, of rack.
Android bodies now share the front window with beige mannequin,
fire in the aisle, domino scatter, assisted living moratorium,
air raid protocol cut with pregnancy facts in lavatory pamphlet.

The endless cataloguing of details as to remember/forget.
Archaic speakers will soon attain the same hush frequency
as Honda criminals thumb stacks of hush money
as young dreamers pour borrowed rum into Slush Puppies.

The wolf moon makes white the rows of the apple orchard.
The dwarf trees sing of supernatural being in overdrive sonatas.
The white horses are loose but they have only nibbled the pond edge
and I am hopeful this is the year where you crawl to my door and lick.

THE NOISE PALACE

Immense coils in the aggravated neighborhood.
The fire of the red building was thrown on the church
and the church was vertical with flames, now just a façade,
blue sky through the arched windows. People say Wow.
They have scribbled Marzipan Latte on a window page
and among the orange dumptrucks we discuss
the precession of the equinoxes.

The Temple of the Vedic Planetarium.
A woman will say you were a demigod
but are now moving backward,
hence all the friction in the mortal realm.
The spectrum of noise has been elucidated by YouTube.
White for calming song of calibrated machines.
Pink for the soft hypnosis of the living earth.
Brown noise for pink noise with more resentment.

The radiators are timed to knock. The universe is a gigantic screw.
Awaken to vision of dancing fire amid the bronze and glass instruments.
The music is not unlike snow against country window, windthrown.
The tinnitus is the interdimensional spiral thread to the top heaven.
The two lines meet to make a point and that point is a circle.
It is on the third day of the year when it is obvious she has no friends.

THE BEDS AND TRAMS OF LISBON

The beds and trams of Lisbon,
calibrated miscreants in the domain of the highway song.
There are five or so people you consistently believe
have perfect lives. Back on the dentist's chair,
back on the phone, fresh from the recitation of the hotline.

The family is doomed.
Anxiety paralysis and the indifference
so powerful it becomes an active force,
a planet maker and eater, the rail switch,
morning chimes at the ice cathedral.
DNA blotches, genetic has-been,
a liquor store closed on Christmas.

THE BROKEN OVUM

The lonesome apartment dogs of New Year's Day.
The animal kings wailing in their material emptiness.
The broken ovum of the floating red empress.
Elaborate textile funerals fill the street of sinister moisture.

Harps dusted with cinnamon are played in the sun spears.
No one is saved on the yellow shore of the regional lake.
The neighbors have returned only to drop things.
Sentient hasps make percussive taunts on the red barns of the valley.

Decisive loss in the geological model and splatter.
When I opened the drawer I was not surprised to find a booty of fangs.
You insist on becoming more beautiful on the balconies of Santiago.
I refuse to treat our romance like an everyday career pyramid.

Cannabinoid and melatonin and dreams of the benevolent aged.
Charging the cut acidtab with the mookaite.
Repetitive actions damned by the reversed eight of pentacles.
Silence achieved in the finishing of the third cup of coffee.

Opening Auden to find him speaking of my birthday (2/12).
Wording my question correctly so I can find the Swedish flag.
Falling asleep beneath the pulse loops of the night helicopter.
Finding my favorite numbers all over the place, meaning nothing.

THE STARBLUR

Corrupt ovaries in the starblur.
Correct overthrows in the cored hole,
axial enigmas betwixt two isomers of zero color.
Fountains of geometrical water,
mafia soldiers rolling black quarters on checkered cloth,
the right breath pattern activates the inane formative pictographs,
the cells inside the cells and the energetic confetti
of the atomic massacre, an Altoid case for every erratum.

Studious and glib and the rotational glyptic,
stone smooth clockwork turning that frees the loaded beam.
You would be amazed at how many times
I have turned you off. Aquatic and invasive plants
finding paths to fulfill in the shimmer cloud.

THE UNGULATES

Individual ospreys
on the coriander plateau.
Gestalt time flashes.
Dawn alone in the room
of metropolitan darkness.
Thinking of
the change mechanism
an ancient city of neurons
fundamental, broken.
The ungulates are in estrus.

THE MIRRORLESS CAMERA

When the time arachnid finally insides me the poison
I will perfectly recite the code of the anonymous ronin
and explain myself to a cousin on a Tokyo street.
Her windows even reminded me of Japanese screen,
the trees watered and sculpted ink
to make the inherent dark veins of photographed nebulae
on lavender panels, it is always this bright,
and the host may be a sex addict.

You sound extra afraid today hailed by melting snow.
Quipping rude clerks, you never run out of jokes huh?
Left to her nipple, gentle and licking,
I dream of mirrorless cameras on stands
arranged in the shape of an amphitheater
but I cannot see the object of their vision.
It is natural to postpone the date of the seppuku.

SHE IS SEQUESTERED

She is sequestered with her twin grey ghost dogs.
She does drape herself in electric silk.
She has drawn the aleph in the soil of the orchid.
She is humble. She is ruthless and crowned.
She throws black di. She rotates ice in heavy vessel.
She has come here through immaculate circumstance.

Her breasts remain barred by exorbitant fabric.
Her library contains the secret tomes of the interpenetrate age.
Her mute decrees are emphatic. Her eunuchs are stoic.
Her black telescope is aimed between the stars.

She makes a jester of the philosopher.
She makes the jester a geometer.
She has put cold presses to the eyes of wolves.
She has put her red fingerprint to the brows of the newborn slaves.

She hibernates in bare cathedrals of striated jade.
She is the ever-sharpening intersection
    of letter of number of image of memory of fantasy of animal.
She is the reigning chieftain drunk on virginal blood spiced
    with reptilian milk.
She is the emergent snake-epiphany of your last comforting dream.
She is the arbiter of realities. She is cloaked in scarlet raven feathers.
She turns the hovering sun stone by circling her right forefinger
    in the black moat.
She is the lubrication of the moratorium and the mausoleum of usurper.
She sleeps in orgasmic realms of which you are only one figment,
    and fast lessening, and fast eroding, and fast melting.
She is the contour and schematic of the haunted memory palace.
She is the collection of ideal and template and archetype
    in marble hall, in forested dome, in ethereal circuitry.
She is the recruiter of drones and the steam of dying lungs.
She is the sensate grid of malignant curvature, of sporadic edge.
She is the long chain of 9s. She is the pupiled cindercone
    from which language blows.
She is incarnate nonexistence and the harrowing lineage
    of the decimal point.
She is the mark, the solitary gesture, the possibility of the singular.
She is the collapse of the solipsist. She is the banshee thousand.

She is the one tolling bell through the interstices of the millennia tree.
She is the truefalse landscape harvested from cinematic opus.
She has not even awakened to her own ever-exploding potentials.
She is the bismuth and quicksilver bleed as arcade-game warp
    in the intestinal reading of the dead marsupial.
She was the mutant, she is the stray, she makes a recreation
    of my lavender body.
She is the emerald hill of guillotines, the catnip in gauzy pouch.
She is the thwarted sunbeam. She is the turquoise ax of runes.
She is the ghost matter of the decapitated tribes.
She is the collective whimper of the urban behemoth.
She is the alchemical residue of the graveyard of the giants.
She is the harbinger of dimensional diamondreverberate.
She is cayenne pepper beneath the fragile top layer of the bottom lip.
She is the salted parhelion aromas of the vaginal altar.
She is the infinite series of transfers in the horizontal megalith of rails.
She does not want and cannot want and desire
    is only her idiot disciple.

She is the fountain of jaws.
She is the multiplication of the hypnosis rendition.
She is the inward falling cascade of 16bit golden rectangles.
She is the echo of the atomic weapon in the deep bone of nickel.
She is coming. She has arrived. She is asking to have a word
    through its perpetual eye of shattering.

METAL OX

Years of toxoplasmosis
in the year of the Metal Ox
Express longing
Foliate detritus, dendritic Mozambique
Harbinger puzzle and Lego tactic
The tan face of Dominique
You're going off the rails
Inhabited by apocalyptic ranting
In the scatter of glares
In the stone fountain of the fallings of the blue jacaranda
In the tree growing out of the canopy of the tree

THE ULTRASOUND

The current is timeless.
If you exist or existed or will exist
or do not exist you are within it,
you make it by its carriage.
Singular and plural within it and of it,
you are the cut for the water to river,
the cable for the atemporal plasmatic milk,
the spearmint lightning flash
a hint of the untouchable network.
Flockshapes are your letters
the wind is the grammar
the memory in this present the word.
It is all right here, unseen, unwanted, borne.
It is the hypnotic litany of future ghosts.
It is a resplendent language
that speaks in rusted toasters
and pregnant heroin queens
smoking in the red prismatic sparkle of gifted jewel.
Grandfathers reborn in living room dreams,
more upright and extolling
and your attention is an open hand,
a waiting device in the mutated space.
Here you find every iteration of yourself
which is the self that entertains
through purposely botched duplication,
ideas like resurrected titans from the
hyperwhite lagoon at the edge of the endoplanet.
Stated version in precision marble
there are sculpted fists in the ridges of your hair,
heated eyelines in glowing balletic appetites
in scenarios fostered to render the divine child
of sequential ghetto, of lumbering quadrant.
Protracted mimesis, beguiling enemas,
a mysterious fourth in every dream,
becoming lucid and exhibernated
becoming animal and sleepeasy,

the silent delta of regenerative energy continues to branch
remembering all but blessing you
with one or two of its infinite orders,
the epilogue of the photocopied birth certificate,
extracted liquids are now bowing herds in the shale of dawn,
you are required to serve the ohmage,
the vibrational root system, the floating spherical tree,
the fungal vertices and the polygons of ore,
all of it bands on the singular spectrum
that ever expands and never grows,
the numbers are merely the black peaks
of the indivisible range and the mountain lakemirrored,
a calibrated wilderness in the carbon desert,
in the morass of microscopic discovery,
the discoveries made by the tools they pushed
through the dark earth of the one imagination,
though one goes from one million to high noon,
food for our food, nebulae for our pupils,
windchime and domed matrices for the blind,
when the snake is finished with its tail
it becomes a spontaneous pulse
in the first frame of the ultrasound.

THE CANDY FLOSS

Utopian pegasus
extracted from the eighth wall
of the seventh avenue.
Sober Dionysus
huffing vaporpen
and drawing caricatures
at the mall.

There is nothing to show for the loneliness.
There has been no attainment, no clarity of vision.
There is only this, now, again, stone-pathed garden.
Nothing has been seen or learned.
Nothing heard, nothing gleaned.
There are only these afternoons of longitudinal slate,
tropical walks over singes of palm.

The seismic velodrome and the purchase eraser.
Catapulted expectation and the candy floss.
Mirrored extension and the synosis healthy ball.
You learn locations to know where the stuff comes from.
Press conference on new state of reality: change.
The room of singing bowl and orthotic,
metronome and small cubic dioramas of loam.
There is nothing to show, nothing to hold,
as if a lucky feather or protective rock,
the narrow museum of rare gumball machine,
the display case of pinball flipper and sugar brand,
man foaming on gurney in the burnished corridor of the defeated sun.
The embedded rails are golden hair.

THE BLACK CONFETTI

She moves in the distance where the jackals have exploded
the last balloon of black confetti. If God gave you
the complete word the light would storm you
and scatter you so it must come in a rumble of whispers,
in elapsed code, we are hungry again, we are angry again,
the snakes are being pushed through the open window.

On the shelves are the jars that hold the contagion.
I can imagine at some point there was a man named Black Ruby.
When I lose everything I will stand with boxed hands,
closed eyes, in my black suit, I have something,
the birds A circle, someone ate my neighbor's
biscotti, which had arrived in a box, and the note he left
asks the question: Who's the sick fuck?

THE PROGRAM

00 I will present myself as cynical yet optimistic
about the prospects of the future.

01 I will repeat the common and modern phrases
of biological hypnosis:
    It could always be worse.
    Tomorrow is another day.
    At least _____.
    The darkest hour is before the light.
    It is what it is.
    Things will get better.
    It used to be worse in olden times.
    Be grateful.
    The world is what you make it.
    Love is all you need.
    Welcome the pain.

02 Once my cynical/optimistic presentation has been
accepted by friends and family as "realistic,"
I will find the state that allows me to purchase a handgun
with the least amount of hassle.
Death by handgun seems to be
the most effective method of self-obliteration.

03 I will use my savings to rent an apartment in this state.
The reason for the move may require the formation of lies,
the telling of lies. There must be a harmony
of specificity and vagueness.
Utilize the phrase: I want something completely different.
Your bravery and optimism
will force the listener to examine their life
instead of examining yours.

04 The prison dance of bureaucracy will begin,
but I will become a citizen of this state.

05 I will begin to browse local gunstores.
It is imperative that I do not make familiars
who may begin to manifest worry, concern.
Meaning: control sexual impulse: the
most dangerous threat to the program.
Though, paradoxically, it may be necessary to acquire
a sexually transmitted disease,
but a serious one, like herpes or AIDS,
in order to channel the frustrated sexual energy
toward the obliteration of the self.

06 Once the proper paperwork has been collected,
the perfect status attained,
I will purchase the handgun.
I will purchase the bullets.

07 The ownership of the handgun may provide
a life-atmosphere of relief. If so,
meditate on the suffering of this life,
how it has forced you to purchase
a highly developed weapon
[compared to what?]
in an arbitrary territory.
Life can provide no lasting peace.
It confuses, deludes, and drugs.
It assaults you with noise.
It exacts immaculate punishment.
It blooms a poisonscape of false hope.
It dilutes past suffering
so further suffering is ensured.
It uses the bodymind for its own
obscure, malignant, and indifferent
desire.

08 Come to understand
that the world beyond death
may contain further suffering
but this is to be embraced
as there is also the possibility
that it contains less.
Here, there is only suffering.
The prospect of less suffering *here*
is part of the invincibility of suffering.
Though death may be part of *here*.
There is the very real possibility of no escape.
But, forward.

09 Eat what you want. Get fat.
A disgusting body will increase
the hatred of the self by the self
and make firm the determination
to obliterate the self.

10 Abstain from drugs.
This includes alcohol.
Inebriated states may lead to sloppy behavior.
Familiars may come to know
your true design, your true aim.
Police may become involved, health
professionals, doctors.
Beings hypnotized by life,
who hope to ensnare you in life.

11 Though it began at birth,
and perhaps in the womb,
begin the process of ending.
This may be called "saying goodbye."
See that all beings here are afraid
and attempting to infect you
with their own particular program,

which is the program of further living,
which is the program of hope,
which is often a disguised deathprogram
but predicated on the deaths of others
instead of the self.
The loss of hope is also a program.
The obliteration of the self is also a program.
The obliteration of the self is also a hope.
The self is a program, is a hope.
Program = Force = Virus.
See the paradox of this vale of suffering.
See the infinite regress.
See the infinite growth.
See the unstoppable thwarting.
See the immense going, the total hunger.
See the winds within the homunculus,
the forest of machinery inside the wind.
See the void chapter.
See the paneled dog feces in the metropolis bacterium.
See the habitual despair.
See the habitual hope.
See the habitual habitual.
See the bitch pummeled by the bloodwolf.

12 Maintain an existence of simplicity.
Simplicity will illuminate the goal.
The goal is the exit/end of this world.
World, which may also be called
    life
    existence
    vale
    veil
    prison
    ghost chamber
    punishment zone
    hell

    molecular tyranny
    evolutionary vipernest
    eternal carrot-before-mule
    the great circle

13 When beings try to convince you
of the miracle, gift, and/or majesty of this world,
remember that this is a cruel condition of your world:
to be surrounded by those that like it here,
and deem it "good," "worthwhile," or even "nothing."
Though pain is not nothing.
Beware the talk of progress or mindfulness
or gratitude or the ascension of the spiral ladder.
Ignore talk of your bodymind not being your own.
If someone says this, respond with
Give me ten thousand dollars, as I am simply
another aspect of the collective worldsoul.
Say this with humor, do not give it a serious tone.
No one must worry about you.
No one must even think about you.

14 Life will begin to rebel.
There will come romantic montage.
There will come fantasies of good health, much wealth.
There will come daydreams of utopian landscapes.
There will come the onslaught of prospective cures.
There will come the design of a neutral peace,
an at-homeness, promulgated by ciphers.
There will even come the idea of the ability
to overcome any of life's myriad challenges
through some sort of permanent adaptability
through some sort of stoic heroism
through some sort of indifferent intelligence.
The idea of respectability will arise,
so your grim determination will attain respectability,
the currency of one shift of the biohypnosis.

15 References to soldiers, prisoners, mothers,
fathers, saints, antisaints, rebels, poets, generals,
genocide survivors, divine children,
historical ideals, and fictional characters
will be made. They must be made.
Suffering will be presented as a hurdle
instead of an infinite desert of broken
glass and venomous snakes,
which transforms into a rose garden
when you become immune to broken
glass and venomous snakes
and become allergic to roses in garden arrangements
[rose gardens].

This will usually be accompanied by sayings ~
    Buck up.
    Pull your head out of your ass.
    Life is what you make it.
    Suffering is a choice.
    Misery is a choice.
    Life is what you make it [again].
    Happiness is a choice.
    Free will is a thing.
    We are spirits having a human experience.
    You never know what's around the corner
    [actually we do: pain, confusion, strife,
    platitudes in the genre of hope].

Beings will also begin to list the ways
they have suffered, or the ways their ancestors have suffered,
or the way beings like animals and trees have suffered,
they will in fact begin to prove
that this is a dimension of suffering and pain
and war and rape and illusion and catastrophe
but of love and salt and puppies and flowers and plumbing
and then they will look at you with eyes of desperation
expecting you to recant all, rest easy, and proceed
[with what?]

now that you know that every being throughout the planet,
and throughout time, has in fact suffered more than you
[except maybe beings in the future?
how long is the future, and how many beings in my
barometer? league? aquifer? spectrum?
of suffering
does it contain?].
This line of thinking is supposed to elicit gratitude,
but instead describes the beguiling nature of suffering.

16 Polish the gun. Care for the gun.
Learn how to use the gun. It may be necessary
to pray to the gun, to worship the gun,
to admire the contours of the gun,
to give the gun a name using a
secret self-created alphabet,
one whose letters resemble trees.

17 The design of death will begin.
Sex without the threat of pregnancy
and disease. Food without the gain of fat.
The ability to remain amazed.
A landscape of *increasing* beauty
and strangeness, without the
insect arsenal, the bad water,
why do we have to pay for pleasure?
With flesh and sleep, with time.

18 A problem will arise.
In the world of death, do you prefer
an improved pleasure scheme,
or the cessation of desire,
the cessation of all desire
forever and always, which may mean
that desire is both activated and extinguished
simultaneously
in a fiery blur of time and space.

19 Another problem: Boredom.
The primary villain. The ein sof.
The black sunmoon. The fanged monster.
A deepening of pleasure may be needed,
mystifying trances and developments
where boredom is not possible,
when its shadow falls
the pleasure only becomes more complex,
more total, yet more surprising.
It can get better and better and better and
better and better and better and better…

20 Hold this idea. Hold the imagery.
Fix the sensation in your bloodsystem,
your tomb of bodymind.
Beware spiritual jingoists.
Beware the fine ass of the checkout girl,
or finish inside it, but never lose
the throne-image of the goal,
the destination of perfect pleasure
and no desire. Lay the handgun
on the pillow beside your head
so that its dark eye greets you in
the blue granular veil of the morning.

21 Go to the steppe, the plains,
go to where the ancestors howl,
where the antelope are deer
and caribou, where the animals
bow to the blonde grass, where the
water shivers in pools, blue frost in the grass,
wait there by the tree made desirous
and reaching by the wind of the seasons,
by the violence of the air and empty turning,
discard your raiment and clutch the gun,
clutch the gun in the vast cold,

remember the destination, remember
the realm of dreams of your return,
wait there by the ghost of the scream of the tree
wait there for the man of the blue dawn
who started all this pain and suffering
who has put you here in this world of confusion
who has watched the years of stalking
and of blandishment and empty cleaning
who has put you with the dust and the mold
the hunger and the poison and the hope
wait there by this tree in the blast of emptiness
and when the slender arrow comes into your heart
and you spit black blood to the frost of the first light
release this phase of grievance and wilderness
know this true pleasurevoid in the morning wind
as the tension is scattered down the tilted world
as the weapon falls to the crystallization
as the final deadtrail of white seed is left on the earth
as the distant form of the man is a shadow
and the sun is coming but is not yet here
and the blood is a cascade and a pool
and the pool is already starred with ice
as the late birds are in v to the south.

Michael Borth is a writer from The Hudson Valley. His work appears in *New World Writing, Fence, Spectra Poets, SELFFUCK, Forever Magazine, DFL Lit, Angel Rust, Expat Press, The Write Launch,* and elsewhere. He is the author of *The Health Department,* a novel published through The Coastlands (thecoastlands.net).

www.ingramcontent.com/pod-product-compliance
Lightning Source LLC
Chambersburg PA
CBHW022126090426
42743CB00008B/1018